RUNNING A MUCK

A BUNCH OF ZANY CARTOONS
by JOHN CALDWELL

D0830372

Writer's Digest Books   •   9933 Alliance Road   •   Cincinnati, Ohio 45242

Library of Congress Cataloging in Publication Data

Caldwell, John, 1946-

Running a muck.

1. American wit and humor, Pictorial.

I. Title.

NC1429.C22A4 1978   741.5'973   78-17835

ISBN 0-911654-60-7

9933 Alliance Road
Cincinnati, Ohio 45242

For Diane—
who gives me love and keeps my Dion records static-free

Acknowledgments

Grateful acknowledgment is made to the following publications for permission to reprint cartoons appearing originally in their pages:

Campus Life—pages 15, 35, 50

Cavalier—page 28

Esquire—pages 8, 14, 17, 22, 26, 42, 54, 62, 64, 65, 66, 74, 80, 111

Medical Economics—pages 7, 113, 114

Mother Jones—pages 63, 106, 107, 112

National Lampoon—pages 12, 19, 20, 32, 33, 36, 67, 88, 102, 103, 109, 110

Oui—pages 25, 30, 31, 101, 125, 126, 127

Saturday Evening Post—page 76

Writer's Digest—pages 11, 21, 23, 27, 29, 47, 104, 108, 116

"Fremont, no one is interested in seeing your slides."

"Pre-minstrel cramps!"

"And at 49 bucks a lesson, you won't be getting many more!"

"Uh, how many vasectomies have you done, Doctor?"

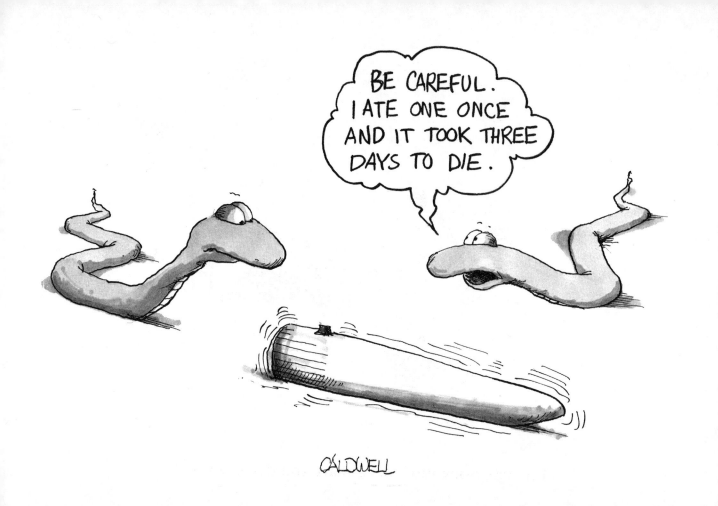

"Coff!"

CALDWELL

SURE YOU CAME FIRST... YOU ALWAYS COME FIRST... THAT'S WHY I NEVER COME AT ALL.
CALDWELL

THE CLEVER AND DANGEROUS HAT SMUGGLER WAITED PATIENTLY FOR HIS AMERICAN CONNECTION.

"You have the right to remain silent. . . ."

IMMENSE BUCK-TOOTHED SNAKE OF UNKNOWN
ORIGIN. HIS SIZE DRAMATICALLY ILLUSTRATED
ABOVE.

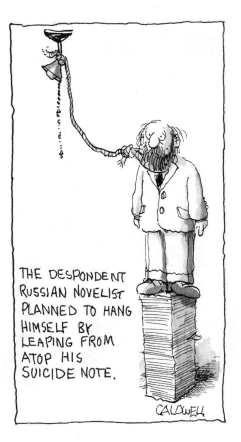

THE DESPONDENT
RUSSIAN NOVELIST
PLANNED TO HANG
HIMSELF BY
LEAPING FROM
ATOP HIS
SUICIDE NOTE.

CALDWELL

CALDWELL

CALDWELL

"Listen, Kid, nine times out of ten it's better to have loved and lost. . . . Much better."

"Officer, I'm afraid I've committed a ghastly crime."

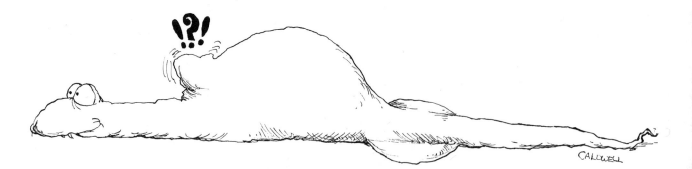

THE **BEAVER VIPER**, FOUND MAINLY
IN CANADA, STUNS ITS PREY
WITH A BARRAGE OF PROBING
QUESTIONS AND DEVOURS THE
HAPLESS BEAVER IN MID THOUGHT.

CALDWELL

"Yes, yes, here's your goddamn money! Now go away!
Can't you see I'm a busy man?"

CALDWELL

CALDWELL

"Good evening, dog lovers, everywhere. . . ."

"It's a forest out there, Cameron!"

"That was not your ordinary run-of-the-mill monarch butterfly, Leo."

"I've come for your fleas."

"A two-buck cigar? Big deal! For your information, pal, this chapeau set me back twice that much."

"Here you go, Rags. I went over it with a fine-tooth comb . . . meat and meat byproducts. Not a speck a cereal."

"It *is* a paper plate. I'm the patron saint of fast-food franchises."

"OK, let's suppose Maurice and I agree to this little enema caper. . . .
Just how many peanuts are we talking about here?"

SSSSSSSS

BUG SPRAY

CALDWELL

"Hey, Mac. How about a dime? I'd like to check in with my answering service."

BEWARE OF THE ~~DOG~~ SNAKE

CALDWELL

ELEVATOR HEELS

CALDWELL

"How do I know you won't spend it on a massage?"

"Hey, this thing is really in there good, huh?"

"Sterno. . . . Sterno. . . ."

THE SLOW WITTED SLOTH PROVED NO MATCH FOR THE SLY AND EVER-PLAYFUL OTTER.

CALDWELL

CALDWELL

"By the grace of the almighty! It is he! It is our sire at last!"

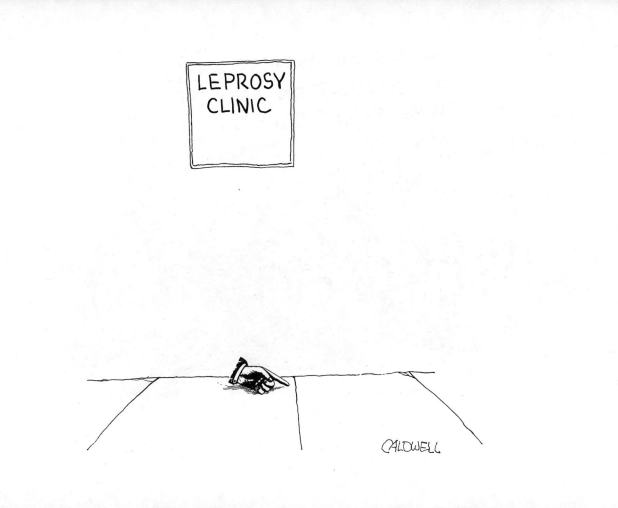

YOU HEARD ME RIGHT. YOU GUYS STINK... WE CAN SMELL YOU ALL THE WAY OVER HERE... WHY, I BET YOU GUYS CAN'T EVEN PICK UP A SPOON,... C'MON LET'S SEE YOU PICK UP THAT SPOON... HAH...
CALDWELL

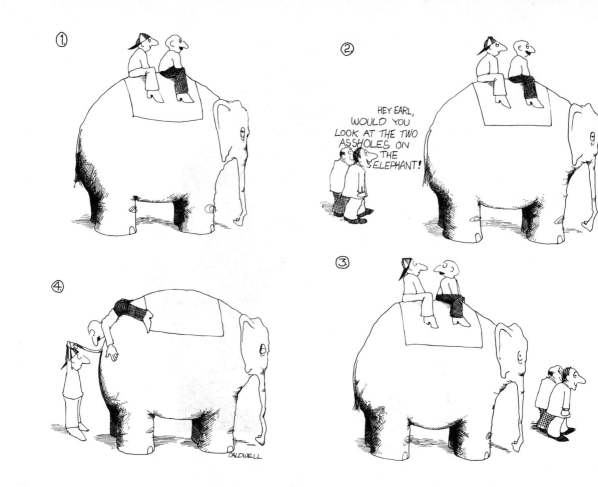

"It's a chafing dish. I'm out of silver bullets."

"Everybody back! This man's swallowed his nose! Don't panic,
I'm a sheet metal worker! Someone bring me a pail
of water and a catcher's mitt!"

"Well, there goes our last coconut, Maurice! I hope you're satisfied!"

"Kiss me . . . . I'm an enchanted basketball player."

"Now there's a subject I'd like to pursue."

"OK, we talked it over. We'll cringe and cower all through it.
But no blueberry hoop! The blueberry hoop is out! We're no fools.
You set up the blueberry hoop and we walk! You got that?"

"We'd like to report a stolen car."

"... Hoo-hoo-hoo-hee-hee-ha-ho-ho-ha-ha-ha-ha. ..."

ACCOUNTING IN THE ROUND.

CALDWELL

"I'm warning you. Don't try anything funny."